**How to Clear Your Mind
Declutter Your Thoughts
Stay Focused on the Prize**

7 Day Jumpstart

To keep your mind clear we must first adjust the way you think and how you go about your day. The first part of this book is a plan to help you move forward. We will start with seven things that you can implement in the first seven days of your change give you a proper foundation for clearing your mind and de-stressing.

In the following pages we will first go over:
    Growing Kindness
    Creating a Sacred Place
    The Benefits of Movement
    Finding Space in Our Own Minds
    Puting Our Feelings in Check
    Savoring the Little Things
    The Benefits of Minimalism

Growing Kindness

Being a kind person has all kinds of health effects. On top of reducing stress by reducing anger, finding ways to be more kind will give more satisfaction from tasks. Think about, you've never felt bad for holding open a door for someone. You've never felt bad for buying a friend lunch or for giving someone an extra complement.

There are six ways that Kindness will affect your everyday health:

- Healthier Heart - Being kind can actually affect the chemical balance of your heart. Positive "feel good" emotions benefit us exponentially. Acts of kindness release the hormone oxytocin inside your body. According to Dr. David Hamilton, oxytocin causes the release of a chemical called nitric oxide in blood vessels. Nitric Oxide dilates (expands) the blood vessels of your heart. This reduces blood pressure. Oxytocin is known as a 'cardioprotective' hormone because it protects the heart.

- Live Longer - According the Health.com you will live longer if you have a stronger, larger, network of friends and family. Being Kind will help you to grown this group of friends and family. Kindness attracts others.
- Stress Reduction - Acts of Kindness will reduce stress. Helping others forces you outside of yourself and your own wants and needs. It creates a better outlook on life.
- Kindness Prevents Illnesses - Diabetes, cancer, chronic pain, obesity, and migraines are all caused by inflammation. Oxytocin, which we discussed earlier, helps to reduce inflammation and thus lowers the chances of diabetes, cancer, chronic pain, obesity, and migraines.
- Feel Good Hormones - Being kind releases feel good hormones like serotonin.
- Eases Anxiety - Easing your anxiety can be difficult for people.

Often times people become sour or mean when they suffer from anxiety. Being kind redirects our thoughts away from what may be causing us to become anxious and allows us to feel good about something instead of being overwhelmed.

Creating a Sacred Place

Create a place where you can be alone. This would be a place that is 100% you. Walking in you would have a sense of ownership and control over it. Establish this as your place, free of the stressors of the outside world.

Here are a few ideas to get you started:
- Place a beautiful piece of fabric on the shelf or table. Pick a color or pattern that calms you.

- Use Incense or essential oils. The use of scent is a powerful way to define a space and can make it calming and enjoyable. Find a scent that causes you to recall a happy memory.

- Add an inspiring image. This can be a photo of nature or someone who inspires you or any object that is beautiful to you. Motivational posters are great for this.

- Light tea lights—our favorite are made of beeswax. Turn off the lights and let the flicker of warm, soft light ease you into a relaxed state.

The Benefits of Movement

Yoga has been shown to reduce stress and anxiety, improve symptoms of depression. It can also increase feelings of optimism and well-being. Try including Yoga in your morning routine. It only takes a few minutes.

Exercise can not only center your thoughts but it will help your body function better reducing stress overall. For many, lifting weights is a time for them to center their thoughts or escape the stresses of life and focus on the task at hand. When you are focused on running or lifting something it's hard to be preoccupied by stressful thoughts.

Finding Space in Our Own Minds

Find space inside your own mind. For many of us our thoughts are like a race track. We keep going around and around repeating the same twists and turns. We all need a place to go outside of that line of thought. Research has shown that learning to identify less with thoughts and feelings by noting them as they come and go can reduce the intensity of feelings of stress and worry by up to 50 percent. Meditating can help us to train our brains to clear themselves.

How to meditate:
- Sit or lie comfortably. You may even want to get a meditation chair or cushion.
- Close your eyes.
- Make no effort to control the breath; breathe naturally.
- Focus your attention on your breathing and on how your body moves with each inhale and exhale. Notice the movement of your body as you breathe. Observe your chest, shoulders, rib cage, and belly. Simply focus your attention on your breath without controlling its pace or intensity. If your mind wanders, return your focus back to your breath.

Puting Our Feelings in Check

Make a habit of taking the time to check in with your feelings and see where you are at emotionally throughout the day. Do you wake up in the bad mood? Why? Let's fix that.

You may identify that there's something constantly upsetting you in the afternoon. Something you can fix or redirect your thoughts towards.

Once we identify bad thoughts we are having we can work on ways to redirect them. This will help to clear the bad thoughts from our minds.

Savoring the Little Things

How often do you make time to stop and smell the roses? When do you take a second to enjoy the good moments? Or, are you just moving from one moment to the next without really experiencing the good parts.

Remember to shake off the bad things and embrace the truly positive things.

The Benefits of Minimalism

  Clear your calendar. Many of us are so caught up in the day to day operations of our own lives that we can't stop ourselves from becoming obsessed with keeping to our schedules. Then we do ourselves one great disfavor, by filling every space we have with "important tasks". Our minds then are filled with the need to move from one moment to the next to accomplish tasks and be at a variety of appointments.

Building on the Foundation

    Now that we have a foundation we can build on it with more tips and tricks to clear our minds and declutter the pile of thoughts we all carry through life.

Declutter

This may seem too simple, declutter your surroundings. Whether it be at home or at your workspace. Have a place for everything, everything in its place, and have a system for where things can be put and found quickly. If disorganization is around you, coupled with an inability to find what you are looking for, you will experience undue stress.

Break things down into small and manageable tasks.

Jobs and to do lists can feel overwhelming when we think only about the end result. If we break tasks down into smaller and more manageable steps, we feel like we are accomplishing something multiple times opposed to once. This makes forward progress more enjoyable and our goal seem more obtainable.

Learn to say "no."

We fear letting people down, upsetting our boss, your friends, your family. We struggle to say "no" and keep piling on more than we can realistically enjoy. Learning to say "no" takes time and may feel rude at first. It becomes easier with practice.

When we say "no," we are allowing ourselves the time to focus on the things we have on our plate. Our priorities. Give your priorities the time and focus they deserve.

Make sleep a priority

We should all be going to sleep at the same time each day and night instead of just, "when we get tired". We should remove all distractions from the bedroom, including our phone screens and t.v.'s that stimulate our minds and keep us awake. Keep Netflix in the living room. Making sleep a priority, allows us to feel sharp and focus for tasks we need to complete. We feel more capable, alert, and more able to perform the tasks at hand, because we are well rested and focus.

Donate things that you do not need

Donating is very cleansing. There is truth to the idea that if you have not worn or used something in a year, you likely no longer have a need for it. There is also the belief that is it does not serve a purpose or make your life better, you can likely live without it.

Declutter your relationships

Step back and take a hard look at who is in your life. Why are they in your life?. Are they mutual relationships? Are both parties benefiting? Do they make you a priority in their lives? If that is the case, cherish them.

However, if not, these might be people worth letting go of. If they are the type of people who never make time for you, frequently cancel plans, make you feel bad about yourself, and only take from others, but never give to the relationship, it is time to consider their role in your life. Consider how your life would change without them.

Reconnect with your creative side

This is telling yourself that you need time for yourself need enjoyable priorities in your life. That you will never allow yourself to be too busy to foster your creativity and get in touch with the younger version of yourself. These exercises can prove extremely cathartic and stress reducing. Painting or drawing can distract the mind from troubles and give you an outlet for frustrations you may not have even realized you were fostering. Writing is another good outlet.

Focus

What you focus on grows, much like a seed. That is an absolute truth. Your thoughts grow based on what you feed them. Be aware of what's going on inside your brain. People today are trying their best to be aware of what they eat. They are probably more aware of this than at any point in our history. They want organic choices and they want healthy foods. They want to cleanse their bodies with "miracle cures". At the same time, they're allowing so much trash to enter their minds.

Look at thoughts and facts going into your mind the same way you look at something going into your body. What are you feeding your mind? Are you spending all day staring at the news and feeling like the world is at the brink of collapse? Do you spend your life on social media? Absorbing post after meaningless post.

Be careful what you're allowing into your brain because it's exactly what will come out of it. If negativity goes in, negativity comes out. If you put in positive thoughts, positive outcomes will happen in your life.

Control your activities

Everyone is busy, but are they getting anything important done? What are you spending your time on? Is it all 100% necessary? Don't mistake activity for progress. Busy work is often unproductive. It's easy to be busy. If you are always busy with mundane tasks you are likely overwhelmed.

It's easy to allow people to pull you in too many different directions. But, do those things contribute to your longer-term goal?

Take charge of your life. Point your focus where it belongs.

Get Clear on your Priorities

Reduce decision fatigue by getting clear on what's important to you. Maybe it's self-care, creativity, or comfort. Whatever your priorities are, use them to help you make decisions and eliminate the mental clutter that comes from trying to decide what to focus on.

If it's not a clear yes it's a clear NO

If it isn't a clear yes, it's a clear no. That's from your clients, friends, family, or yourself. This may seem like a ruthless way to make decisions. You might feel like you are limiting your opportunities. But actually you are committing to opportunities and choosing some opportunities over others. It's a matter of opportunity cost.

Create a System for Ideas

Let's say that your amazing brain is overflowing with ideas. You have too many ideas and thoughts and dreams. So much so that you don't know what to do with them. They're overwhelming you more than helping you because you have too many options. How can we clear this up?

Start by creating a way to store your ideas. Use Google Drive or the notes app on your phone. Stick to one place so you will always know where to find your ideas. The next idea you have, can be saved here for future use. If you ever need it, it's there.

Consume Information in a mindful manner

We consume. If there is anything purely human, it is our appetite for consumption. What we consume we become. We must remember to take in content that benefits our goals. If we are seeking to sell more products online we would benefit more from watching marketing educational content or interviews of successful entrepreneurs.

The truth is, most of the content online or television is not beneficial to you. Most of it will not enhance your set of skills. It is merely meant to entertain or distract you. While some entertainment is good. It is important to not fall into the trap of always needing to be entertained.

Don't be afraid to let go

Give your brain some space by emptying it on a regular basis. Be willing to let go and not engage every little idea or thought you have. Make time in your schedule to get rid of whatever's cluttering up your mind. It is good to make a list of everything that's floating around in my head and just get it all out on paper. Sometimes people do this with journals or paper that they throw away afterwards. But if you visualize it all and get it physically out of your head, you may sleep better and wake up with a clearer mind.

Keep A Journal

Journaling is a great way to relax your mind. Journaling will also help you to analyze and organize your thoughts. Studies have shown that expressive writing eliminates intrusive thoughts about negative events and improves working memory. Researchers believe that these improvements may, free up our cognitive resources for other mental activities. Including the ability to manage stress more effectively. Writing in a daily journal can also help manage anxiety and cope with depression, as it's a healthy outlet to release bottled emotion. You don't have to be a good writer. You don't even have to be average. Just doing it is enough. No one else ever needs to see it.

Avoid Multitasking

It may sound counter-productive but performing multiple tasks at once detracts from the primary task. Your full attention is not devoted to writing a book or creating a marketing plan if you are watching Netflix for 4 hours while you "work". Having a single focus allows you to devote all of your mental energy to the task at hand. Opposed to using having some of your attention dragged away from you by the comedy you put on so you could finally see that season ending while at the same time trying to reformat your company website.

Breathe

Take a deep breath.

Pause.

Exhale slowly.

Repeat.

How does it feel? Great.

Deep breathing is a simple and effective technique that clears your mind, induces tranquility, and can elevate your mood instantly. Deep breathing exercises lowers the heart rate and blood pressure while stimulating the parasympathetic nervous system which helps your body to relax. On top of being a stress reliever, breathing exercises also promote concentration and strengthen your immune system.

Be Decisive

Bing decisive is something that most people lack. It's hard to make decisions sometimes. Other times we know just what to do. Most of the time we know the decision we should make right when it's time to make it. We say we need to think about things because we need to justify the decision to ourselves. Being decisive cuts down the time to make decisions and allows you to throw away the stress of decision making. Trust your gut.

Share Your Thoughts

Talking to a loved one about how you feel is a great way to release pent-up emotions. Sharing your thoughts with others can also help you look at things from a fresh perspective which can help you think clearer and make better decisions.

Limit The Amount Of Media You Intake

The media you consume, T.V., internet, YouTube, Netflix, has a huge impact on your mental health. We spend hours online reading blogs, Facebook, and watching viral videos. The overabundance of information being thrown at you can clog your brain bringing on stress and anxiety.

By limiting the amount of information you consume you are able to get rid of all that media-related clutter lurking around your mind. You can start by setting a limit on the amount of time you spend on social media and T.V. It is also important to avoid negative content. Keeping a positive attitude is essential.

Rethink your sleep

Sometimes when you aren't getting enough sleep or your sleeping patterns aren't ideal you have a foggy mind. Keeping a consistent sleep pattern allows your mind to follow a schedule.

Our bodies are complex machines that enjoy routine. A sleeping routine will help your mind function.

Get in touch with nature

Traveling through nature has a way of calming the senses. Fresh air and getting away from modern conveniences can help you to reacquaint yourself with the natural side of life. We often forget that computers and toilets aren't exactly natural. They are normal to us now but biologically we still have a primal side that connects with the outdoors. A short stroll through a wooded area could be enough to distract you from the pressures of the modern era.

www.ingramcontent.com/pod-product-compliance
Lightning Source LLC
Chambersburg PA
CBHW031514210526
45464CB00007B/2902